A Stepping-Stone Book

How to Make a Cloud

By Jeanne Bendick

Parents' Magazine Press • New York

Copyright © 1971 by Jeanne Bendick
All Rights Reserved
Printed in the United States of America
International Standard Book Number: 0-8193-0441-7
Library of Congress Catalog Card Number: 74-134834

CONTENTS

Look at the Sky 5

Where the Clouds Are 8

Heat Makes Air Rise 16

How to Make a Cloud 18

Different Kinds of Air 30

Clouds Have Shapes 34

Clouds Have Names 38

What Can You Tell from the Clouds? 42

Big, Bad Clouds 50

Directions for Making Different
    Kinds of Rain 52

Directions for Making Snow, Sleet, and Hail   54

Directions for Making Smog 56

Clouds Do More Than Just Rain 58

Cloud Poems 60

Index 63

LOOK AT THE SKY

Sometimes the sky looks all blue.
You can't see a cloud anywhere.

Sometimes the sky looks all gray.
A sheet of clouds covers the blue and
you can't see blue sky anywhere.

But if you went up in an airplane on a day like that, up through the clouds, you would see blue sky everywhere above you and clouds everywhere below. They look thick and white in the sun, like piles of whipped cream or snowy mountains.

WHERE THE CLOUDS ARE

Sometimes clouds are very low. They are low enough to touch the ground.

Sometimes clouds are very high—higher than mountains, higher than some airplanes. But even the highest clouds are not very far from Earth.

Around Earth there is a blanket of air. We call that air Earth's *atmosphere*.

Close to Earth, the atmosphere is thick. There is a lot of air.

The thick layer of air close to Earth is called the *troposphere*.

All living
things on Earth live in the troposphere.
All the weather on Earth is there too.

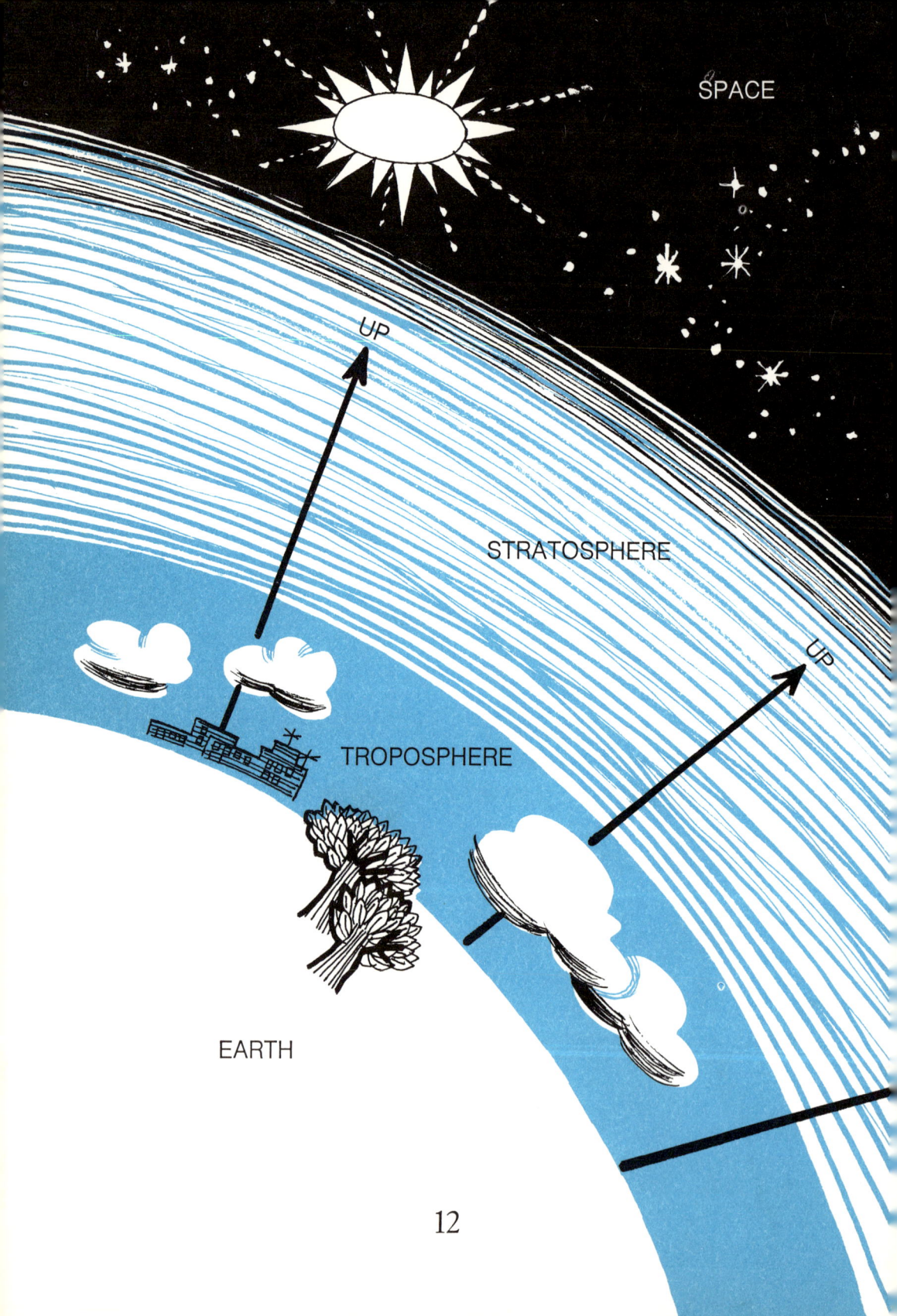

Higher up, the atmosphere is thinner. There is not much air.

This high layer of thin air is called the *stratosphere*.

There is not enough air in the stratosphere for living things.

And there are hardly ever clouds.

Above the stratosphere is *space*. There are no clouds in space. That's because there is no air in space. You can't have clouds without air.

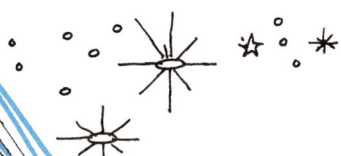

Space is everywhere
outside the stratosphere.
On the round earth
Up also means OUT,
away from Earth.

    Air is real, as real as the Earth.
You can't see air, but you can see it move leaves and papers, flags and branches.
    When it moves, you can feel it blowing.
    And you can feel if the air is hot or cool.

The sun does not heat the air directly.
The sun heats the Earth and makes it hot.

Then the hot Earth heats the air around it.
The hotter the Earth gets, the more it
heats the air close to it.

HEAT MAKES AIR RISE

When air is heated, it goes up. Hot air is light.

Colder air is heavier. It sinks.

It is the same with everything on Earth. Heavier things sink closer to the center of the Earth. Lighter things float on the heavier ones.

It is the same with clouds. Thin, light clouds are high in the sky. Thick, heavy clouds are closer to Earth.

Does heated air always go up?
Some time when the oven is on, open the oven door a little and put your hand in the air over it. How does the air feel?
Now put your hand in the air below the oven door. How does the air feel?
Open the refrigerator door and try the same thing.

Which way does the hot air go?
Which way does the cool air go?

HOW TO MAKE A CLOUD

If you were making clouds, what would you need?

You would start with air. Then you would add some water.

The air is up there to begin with, but where does the water come from?

Try this.

Put a pan of water on the stove and turn on the heat under the pan. Watch what happens.

When the water begins to boil, it turns to water vapor, or steam. The water vapor rises into the air over the pan.

Do you think you can see it?
You can't. You can't see steam, any more than you can see air.

The air over the pan gets hot, and rises. As the air rises away from the hot pan, it begins to cool.

Warm air can hold a lot of water vapor. Cool air can't hold so much.

That's why in the summer, when it's hot, the air is usually more humid—or wetter—than it is in the winter when the air is cold.

When the air rises away from the pan and cools, some of the water vapor from the pan begins to change back into tiny droplets of liquid water. They make a little cloud in the air over the pan.

That's what a lot of people think is steam.
But it's not steam. It's a cloud.

The same thing happens everywhere on Earth. As hot air rises away from the hot Earth, it cools. The water vapor begins changing back to liquid water. Then you see clouds.

Now do this.

Hold a cool, dry, metal spoon in the cloud over the pan of boiling water. (Use a long-handled spoon and be careful. The steam over the pot is hot.) What happens on the spoon? Can you see drops of water?

The droplets have come together on the spoon. They have *condensed* into drops of water. When they get big enough and heavy enough it will rain over the pan.

To make a real cloud in the sky, the droplets must have something to stick to, just as your drops stuck to the spoon.

Some clouds form around tiny bits of ice.

Some clouds form around grains of dust or soot or pollen.

Some clouds form around bits of salt, blown into the air from the ocean.

When water vapor condenses around stuff in the air, you can see a cloud.

There is always water vapor in the air around the Earth.

It comes from ponds and puddles and wet clothes and plants.

It comes from lakes and rivers and oceans.

The sun pulls the water vapor up into the air.

The sun shines on oceans, ponds, and rivers and makes them warmer. The warmer the water gets, the faster vapor goes into the air.
But water goes into the air even when it isn't hot. That's why wet streets and puddles dry up, even in the winter.

Most of the water in the clouds comes from the ocean. Then why doesn't it rain over the ocean and nowhere else?

Before the water droplets in a cloud can get big enough and heavy enough to rain, the air where the cloud is must get cool enough for a lot of drops to come together. The ocean holds heat very well. Any large body of water holds its heat. When the weather is warm, the warm ocean does not get cold enough at night to cool the air over it.

Even when the seasons change, the ocean cools very, very slowly.

The land cools much more quickly.

Clouds do not condense over the ocean unless cold air from land blows over the warm water. What usually happens is that the wind blows water vapor from the ocean over the land, where it is cooled into clouds.

When sailors far out at sea see clouds, they can guess that some kind of land—even an island— is under those clouds.

So to make clouds in the sky you need water, and sun to heat the water so that some of it changes to water vapor and rises into the air.

Cool water vapor into tiny drops

Add salt or dust to make bigger drops

Mix in wind

You need to cool the water vapor so that some of it changes back into droplets of water.

You need something for the droplets to stick to, so that more and more of them can come together and make bigger drops. You need wind, to move the clouds and move the air.

DIFFERENT KINDS OF AIR

    All air isn't alike.
Some is warm and some is cold.
Cold air comes from the north.
Usually it is dry.
Warm air comes from the south.
Usually it is damp, because
it has blown across the warm sea.

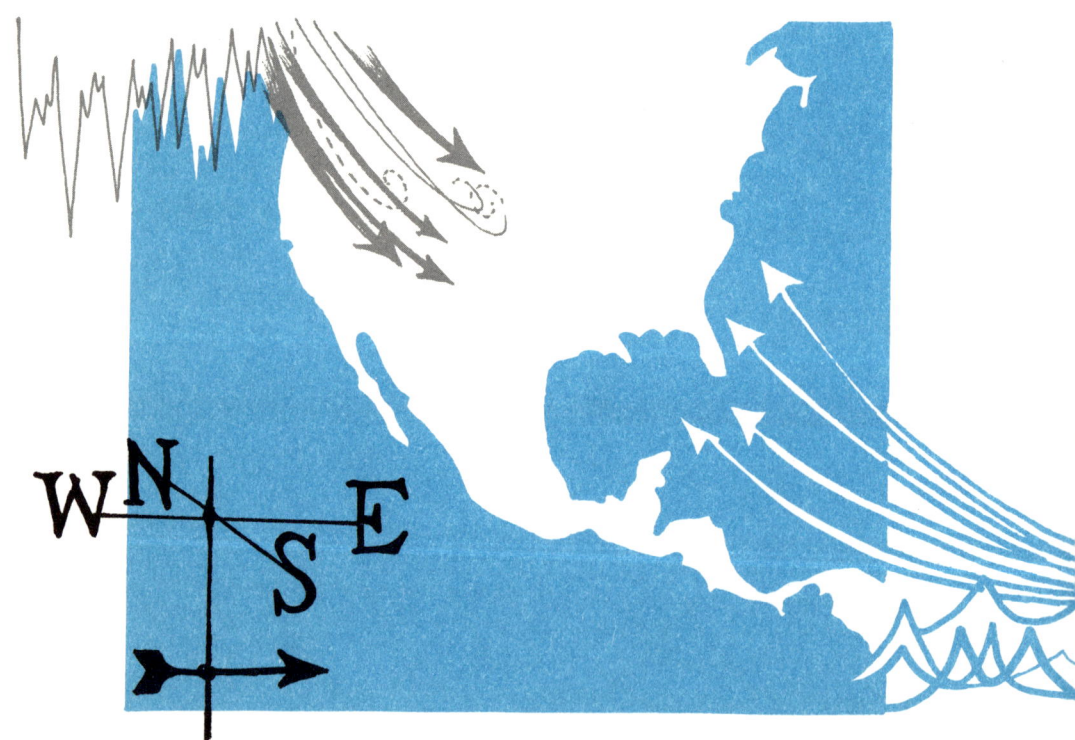

Big masses of cold air travel together.
So do masses of warm air.
They bump into each other.
They push each other.
The place where one kind of air mass meets another kind is called a *front*.

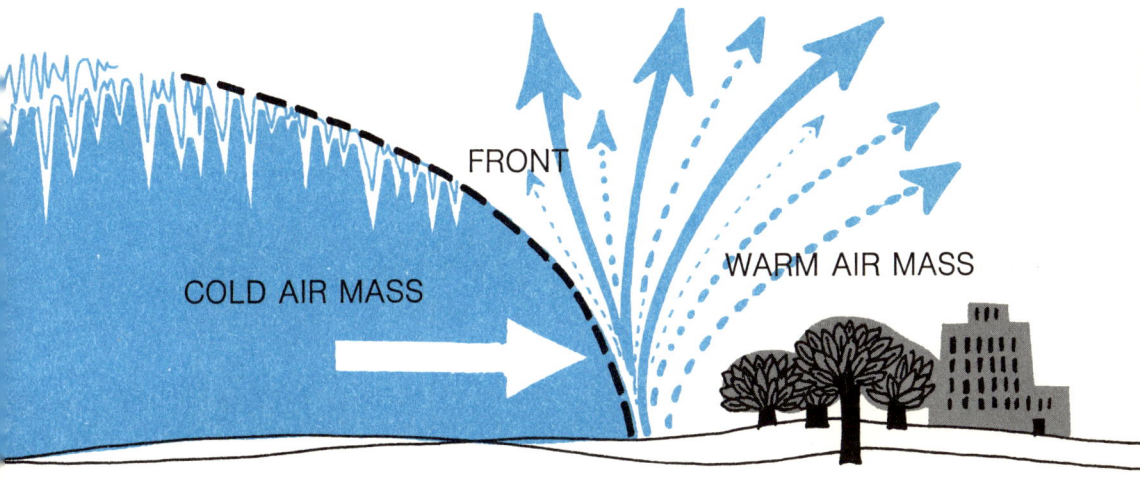

Air masses are big. Some are 500 miles across or bigger. One kind of air mass pushes the other kind out of the way.

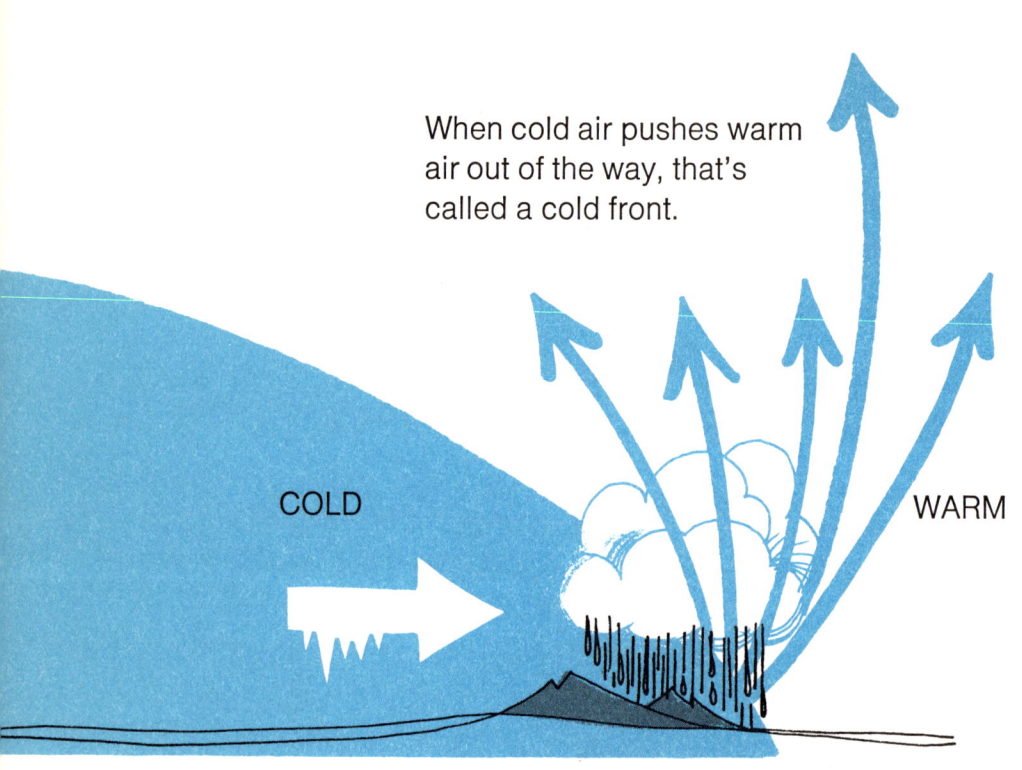

When cold air pushes warm air out of the way, that's called a cold front.

COLD

WARM

When a cold front comes, it pushes in under the warm air mass. Why do you think that happens?

A front makes the weather change. A cold front brings heavy rain that doesn't last long. Then the weather is cool and clear.

When warm air pushes cold
air out of the way, that's
called a warm front.

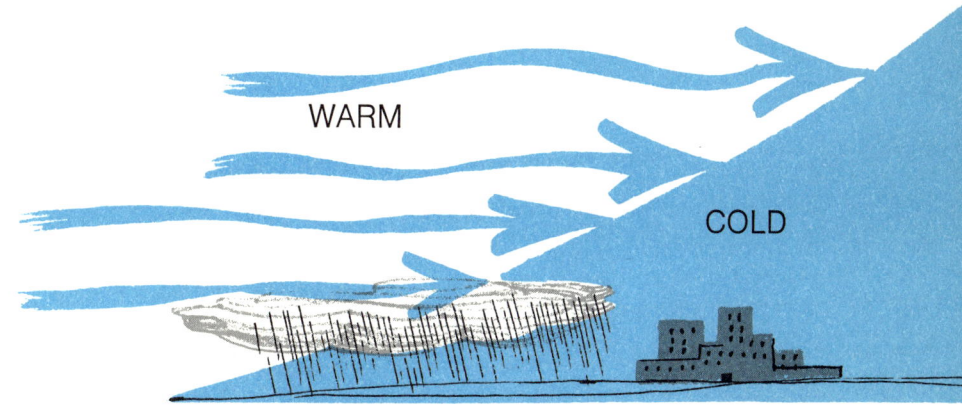

When a warm front comes,
it flows over the top of
the cold air mass.
Why do you think that happens?

A warm front brings drizzly rain that lasts a long time. Then the weather is damp and cloudy.

You can tell which kind of front is coming by watching the clouds.

CLOUDS HAVE SHAPES

When you look up at the clouds from the ground, every cloud seems to have a different shape.

Some nice warm day, when there are a lot of clouds in the blue sky, just lie on your back and watch them.

You can watch from a yard or a field.
You can watch from the park or a bench on the sidewalk.
Sometimes clouds look like
castles and cities,
ships and animals,
monsters and flowers.

The shape of clouds tells you something

Clouds don't just *happen* to be different shapes. The shape of a cloud means something. Different kinds of clouds mean that different things will be happening to the weather.

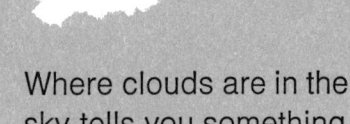

Where clouds are in the sky tells you something

How clouds change
tells you something

Wherever you are in the world,
if you watch the shapes of clouds,
watch where they are in the sky,
watch how they are changing,
you can tell a lot about what the
weather is going to be.

CLOUDS HAVE NAMES

Not every cloud has a name
of its own, like Jill or Bob.
But *kinds* of clouds have names.
They are named by their shapes.

Even though you imagine that you
see many shapes in the clouds,
there are really only three main kinds.

There are streak clouds, that look like
wisps of hair blowing high in the sky.
Weathermen call them *cirrus* clouds.

STREAK CLOUDS

HEAP CLOUDS

There are heap clouds, like puffy piles of cotton. Weathermen call them *cumulus* clouds.

There are sheet clouds, spread out across the sky. Weathermen call them *stratus* clouds.

SHEET CLOUDS

Weathermen all over the world work together to figure out what the weather is going to be. So they all use the same words for talking about clouds.

Like scientists everywhere they use Latin words for naming things.
Cirrus is a Latin word for "hair" or "curl".
Cumulus is a Latin word for "heap".
Stratus means "spread out".

The word *nimbus* means "black rain cloud." When nimbus is added to another cloud name, it tells you what you can expect to happen.

Some clouds are combinations of two kinds.

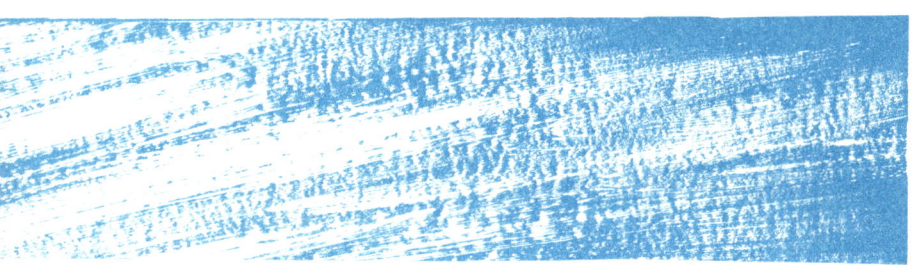

These are cirro-stratus clouds.
Can you see why?

These are cumulo-nimbus clouds.
Can you see why?
When you're hitching cloud names together, it is easier to say "o" in the middle than "us."

CIRRUS

Warm front clouds
start high in the sky.
So, usually you can
tell ahead of time that
the weather will change.
You can see a warm front
coming.

WHAT CAN YOU TELL FROM THE CLOUDS?

Cirrus clouds form very high in the sky, where it is always cold. They are made of tiny ice crystals—frozen water vapor.
Cirrus clouds are warm-front clouds.
Very high ice clouds look like wisps,
or hooks,
or thin veils across the sky.
When the sun or the moon shines through the ice veil it makes a kind of rainbow ring.

Cirro-cumulus and alto-cumulus look alike. "Alto" in a cloud name means high.

CIRRO-STRATUS

Warm front clouds go downhill. But these are all still high clouds.

    Cirro-cumulus clouds are high and frozen too. They look like a skyful of cotton balls close together.
Some people call this a mackerel sky.
    High clouds are new clouds.
They have to get lower,
and older,
and change into other kinds of clouds before they rain.

Cumulus clouds are cold-front clouds. They are lower than cirrus clouds.

These little, puffy cumulus are nice-day clouds. They don't rain.

These bigger, puffy cumulus clouds have knobs and bumps, domes and hills. They hardly ever rain either.

When cumulus clouds get raggedy instead of puffy, they are changing into rain clouds. When they get very raggedy and uneven, closer together and lower in the sky, usually they rain.

In the summer, raggedy cumulus in the morning can mean showers or thunderstorms in the afternoon. But even if the clouds are thick, if they stay high and keep moving, probably it won't rain.

Some cumulus clouds bring more than rain. Another name for a cumulo-nimbus cloud like this is a *thunderhead*. It is very tall with a flat top that leans in the direction of the storm.

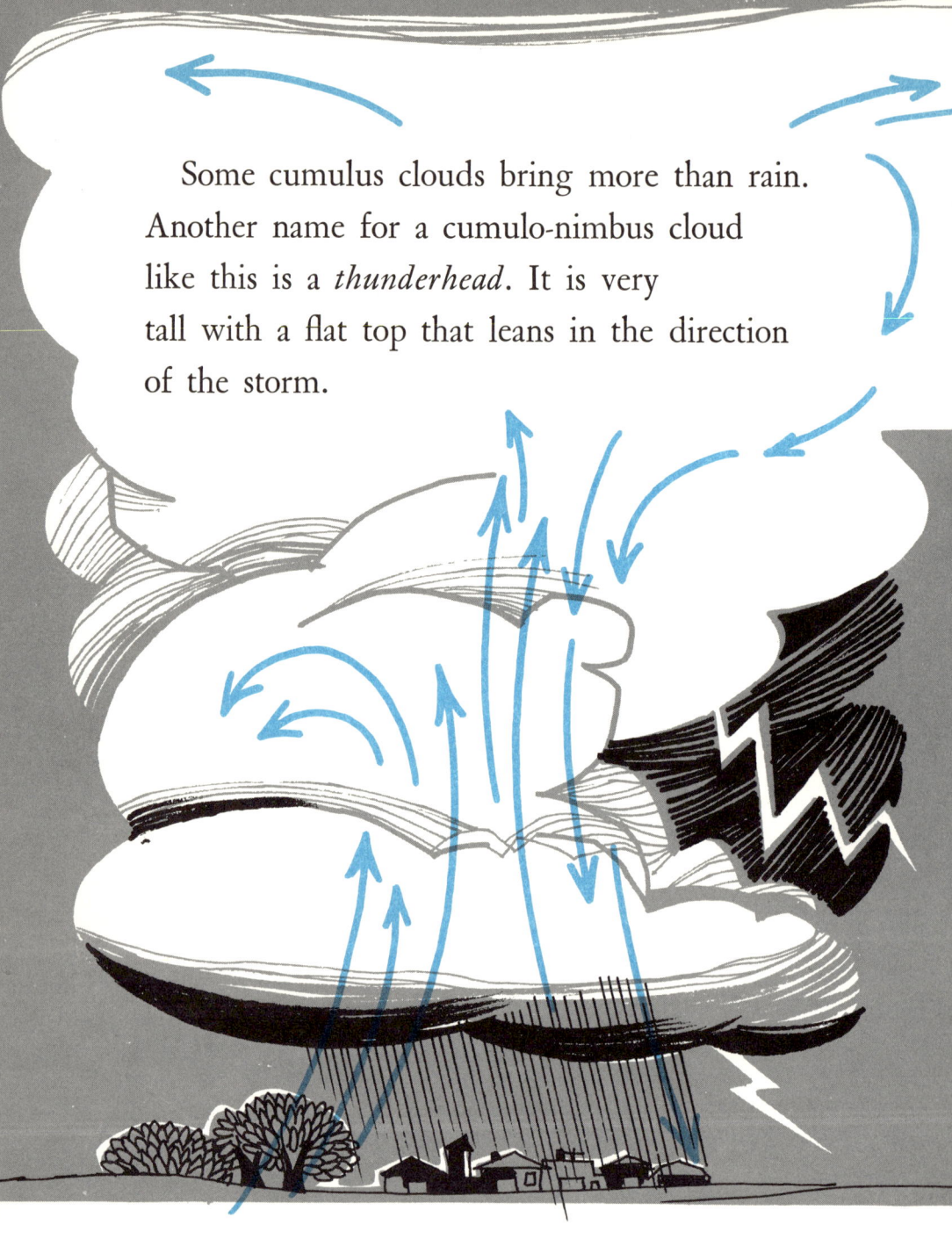

Inside a thunderhead there are strong, hot winds going up and strong, cold winds sweeping down. If the storm strikes, it brings hard rain or even hail, and thunder and lightning.

Cold front clouds move fast. You can't always tell ahead of time that they are coming.

Cumulus clouds like this are called a squall line. They are a whole collection of strong thunderstorms traveling together. A squall moves fast. It doesn't last long but it can be dangerous.

Stratus clouds are warm front clouds.

Very high, thin sheets of stratus clouds don't rain. They are made of ice.
But when stratus clouds get lower and thicker, they tell that a warm front is coming. There are ice crystals on top and water droplets on the bottom.

When the bits of ice fall down into the cloud, the whole cloud gets
wetter
and heavier
and lower. Then it rains or snows.

Stratus makes rain and snow

Stratus makes drizzle

Sometimes stratus clouds are low and thin—only a few hundred feet above the ground. Sheet clouds like this drizzle.

When warm, moist air is cooled very close to the ground or to water, we are right in the cloud we call fog.

Stratus makes fog

BIG, BAD CLOUDS

Hurricanes form over the ocean, when the hot sun shines over the hot, still sea for a long time. The air over the water gets very warm and wet. If cold air blows in then, a hurricane is born. A hurricane cloud blows around in a huge circle, sometimes 600 miles across, making tremendous rains and winds. Hurricanes have different names in different parts of the world.

Hurricane clouds make a wall around the center of the storm. Hurricanes are called typhoons in the Pacific Ocean, cyclones in the Indian Ocean, and willy-willys around Australia.

Tornadoes form over hot land. A dark, funnel-shaped cloud stretches down all the way to the ground, out of a heavy cumulo-nimbus cloud line. It roars and twists and turns and sucks things up through the funnel— even things like cows and trucks. Sometimes, miles away from where the tornado has touched down, it rains frogs and fishes and other small things that were sucked up by the tornado cloud.

DIRECTIONS FOR MAKING DIFFERENT KINDS OF RAIN

Heat some air.

Let it rise.

Mix it with water vapor that the sun has lifted out of lakes, ponds, rivers, and the sea.

Let the air and water vapor mixture rise until it begins to cool.

Put in bits of stuff for the water to stick to, so the drops get big and heavy.

Then add wind.

To get a long rain, blow warm, damp wind against a mass of cold air.

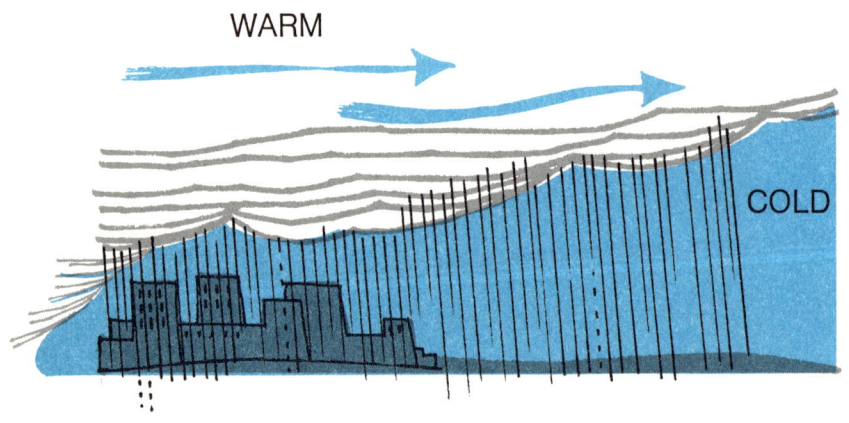

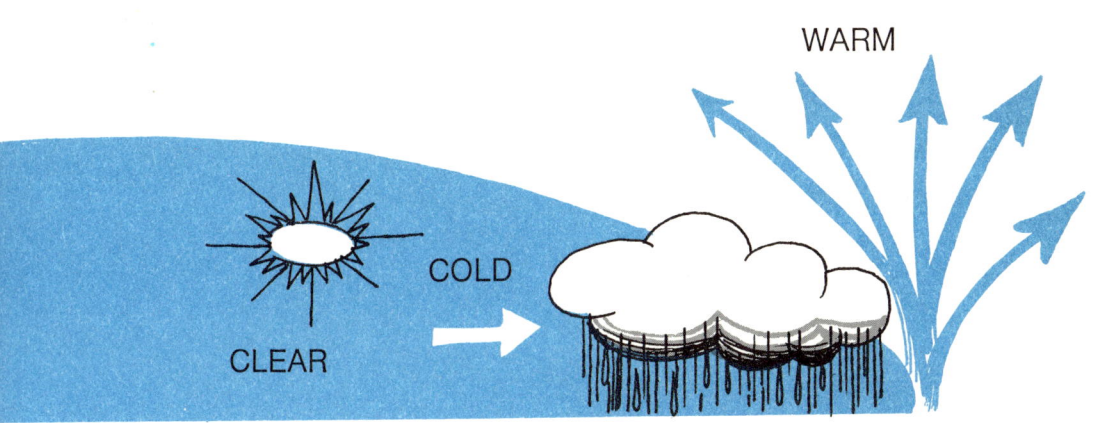

To get short, hard showers, force cold wind under warm air, lifting it away from the ground.

To make a thunderstorm or a hard spring rain with big drops, lift hot air high into the sky, through a mass of cooler air.

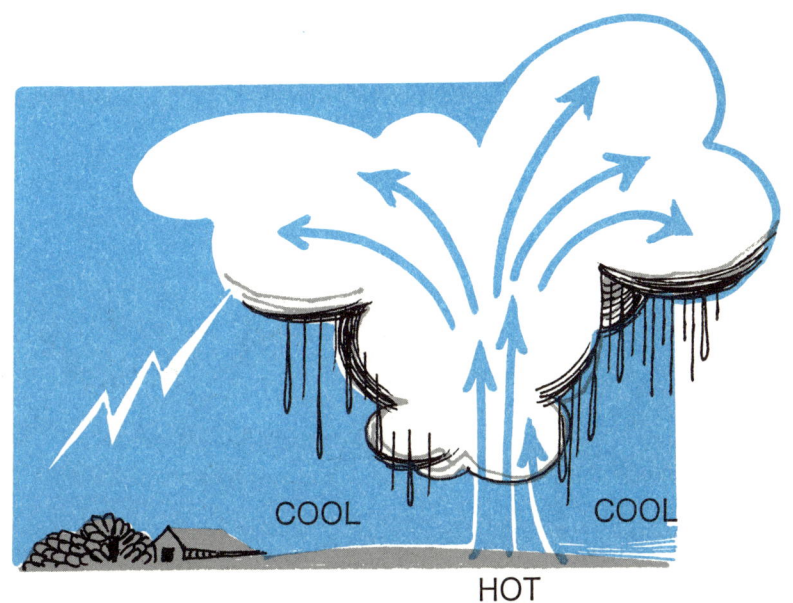

DIRECTIONS FOR MAKING SNOW, SLEET, AND HAIL

To make snowflakes, take cold, damp air and freeze the water vapor as it condenses.

To make sleet, start with rain and freeze it as it falls. To make sleet that stings, add a wind.

To make hail, you will need a lot of strong wind blowing up and down inside a cloud. As big raindrops form and start to fall, the wind carries them up through the cloud, high enough to freeze. Then they fall, and more water condenses around the ice.

If the winds are strong inside the cloud, they will go up and down, up and down, getting new layers of ice each time, until they are too heavy for the wind in the cloud to lift again.

Then the hail falls—sometimes as big as baseballs.

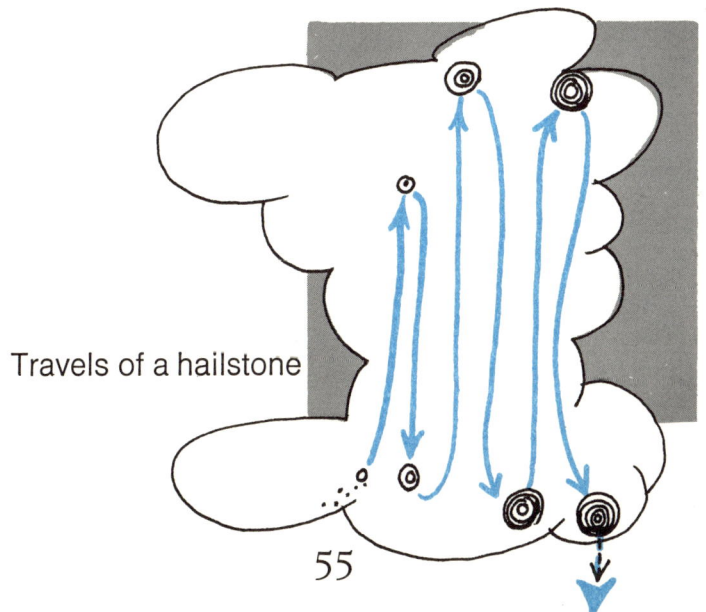

Travels of a hailstone

DIRECTIONS FOR MAKING SMOG

People make smog very well. Clouds of smog hang over almost every big city, and over some smaller ones too.

To make a smog, you need exhaust gases from cars and buses and trucks. Add smoke from factories and incinerators and maybe the fumes of chemicals.

When water vapor condenses around all that junk in the air, it makes a smog.
Smog doesn't rain. It just hangs there, polluting the air we breathe.
In some places it blows away and becomes a part of other clouds that do rain.
In some places it never goes away.
Do you think we should do anything about that?

CLOUDS DO MORE THAN JUST RAIN

Whether the clouds are thin and high or low and thick, they act as a sort of blanket between the Earth and the sun.

The clouds around the Earth catch a lot of the sun's heat and light and reflect it back, out into space.

A cloudy day is cooler than a clear day because so much of the sun's heat never reaches the Earth.

But a cloudy night is warmer than a clear night. At night, when the Earth cools off and the heat rises away from it, clouds keep that heat from disappearing out into space.

On the moon, the days are very, very hot and the nights are bitter cold. Can you guess why?

CLOUD POEMS

A ring around the moon or sun
Means that a change has just begun.

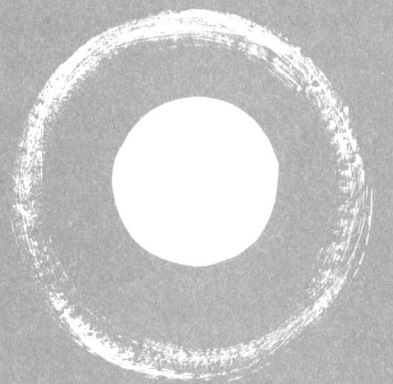

When the mares' tails come together
You will see a change in weather.

When cumulus are round and small
There won't be any rain at all.
When cumulus get rough and gray
It will be a rainy day.
When cumulus begin to rise
You'll see lightning in the skies.

High clouds going one way,
Low clouds 'cross them scurry—
Wind and rain are coming!
Hurry home now! Hurry!

Rain before seven,
Clear by eleven.

INDEX

air, blanket of, 10;
  thick layer of, 10;
  and Earth, 10–11, 15, 21;
  thin layer of, 13
  in space, 13;
  and clouds, 13, 18;
  hot, 14–17, 20, 21, 30, 31, 33, 52, 53;
  cold, 14–17, 20, 21, 25–27, 30, 31, 32, 33, 52, 53, 54;
  in summer and winter, 20;
  and water vapor, 24–25;
  different kinds of, 30;
  damp and dry, 30;
  and hurricanes, 50;
  and fog, 49;
  pollution of, 57;
  warm, *see* air, hot
  water and, *see* water *and* water vapor;
  see also air masses
air masses, 31, 32, 33
alto-cumulus clouds, 43
atmosphere, 10, 13
Australia, willy-willys near, 50

blanket, of air, 10;
  of clouds, 58

cirro-cumulus clouds, 43
cirro-stratus clouds, 41
cirrus clouds, 39, 40, 42, 44
clouds, low, 8, 44, 45, 48, 49, 58, 61;
  high, 9, 42, 43, 45, 48, 58, 61;
  thin, 16, 48, 49, 58;
  thick or heavy, 16, 45, 58;
  how to make, 18–29;
  formation of, 22–23
  sailors and, 27;
  shapes of, 34–41, 43–51;
  names of, 38–41; *see also* individual *names;*
  new, 43;
  poems about, 60–62;
  see also fronts
condensation, 22, 23, 27, 29, 43, 55, 57
cumulo-nimbus clouds, 41, 46, 51
cumulus clouds, 39, 40, 44–46, 47, 61
cyclones, 50

dust, and clouds, 23

Earth, and clouds, 8–9, 16, 58–59;
  and air, 10, 12, 15, 21;
  and weather, 11;
  sun and, 15;
  and heavy and light things, 16;
  and water vapor, 24–25

fog, 49
front, 31;
  cold, 32, 44, 47;
  warm, 33, 42, 48

hail, how to make, 55
heap clouds, 39
heat, and air, 15–17
humidity, 20
hurricanes, 50

ice, and clouds, 23, 42, 43, 48;
  and hail, 55
Indian Ocean, cyclones in, 50

lightning, 47, 61

mackerel sky, 43
mares' tails, 60
moon, weather on, 59

names, of clouds, 38–41;
  see also *individual names*
nimbus, 40
north, cold air from, 30

ocean, clouds and, 26–27;
  and hurricanes, 50

Pacific Ocean, typhoons in, 50
poems, about clouds, 60–62
pollen, and clouds, 23

rain, 22, 62;
  and clouds, 22, 26, 40, 43–51;
  heavy, 32;
  drizzly, 33, 49;
  how to make, 52–53;
  and sleet, 54;
  and hail, 55;
  and smog, 57

sailors, and clouds, 27

salt, and clouds, 23
shapes, of clouds, 34–37, 38, 43–51
sheet clouds, 39
sky, blue, 5, 6, 7;
  clouds in, 5–9, 16, 37, 42;
  gray, 6;
  mackerel, 43
sleet, how to make, 54
smog, how to make, 56–57
snow, 48;
  how to make, 54
soot, and clouds, 23
south, warm air from, 30
space, 12, 13
squall line, 47
steam, *see* water vapor
storms, 50;
  see also thunderstorms
stratosphere, 12, 13
stratus clouds, 39, 40, 48–49
streak clouds, 38
sun, and Earth, 15;
  and water vapor, 24–25, 28;
  and hurricanes, 50;
  clouds and, 58

thunderhead, 46, 47
thunderstorms, 45, 47, 53
tornadoes, 51
troposphere, 10–11, 12
typhoons, 50

water, and clouds, 18–29;
  see also water vapor
water vapor, 19–29, 52, 54, 57;
  frozen, 42
weather, on Earth, 11;
  and fronts, 32–33;
  and clouds, 36–37, 42–47, 58–62
weathermen, 39, 40
willy-willys, 50
wind, 29, 47, 50, 52, 53, 61;
  and sleet, 54;
  and hail, 55

551.6
B
BENDICK, JEANNE
　How to make a cloud

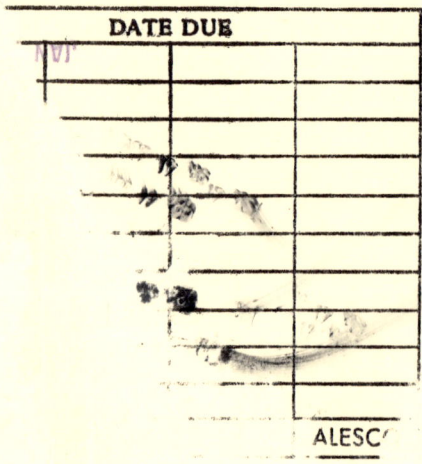